Circle Of Stone
A Kid's Guide To Stonehenge

Photography By John D. Weigand
Poetry By Penelope Dyan

Bellissima Publishing, LLC
Jamul, California
www.bellissimapublishing.com

copyright © 2010 by Penny D. Weigand

All rights reserved. No part of this book may be reproduced or transmitted in any form or by any means, electronic or mechanical, including photocopying, recording, or by any other means, or by any information or storage retrieval system, without permission from the publisher.

ISBN 978-1-935630-37-1

First Edition

For Those who do the Impossible

Circle of Stone
Bellissima Publishing, LLC

Introduction

The area of Stonehenge was long used by the ancients as a burial ground, and you can see the burial mounds today where the ancient people cremated and buried their dead. It is long believed that the Druids constructed Stonnehenge as a place of worship, and Stonhenge is considered to be a great architectural feat. You can walk in a circle around Stonehenge and see it from many perspectives, set in its natural setting with sheep and cattle grazing nearby.

When Stonehenge was built is also up for debate. Some say it was built as early as 3000 BC, others speculate it was constructed about 2400 BC. No one knows exactly how this monument was created or why, and no one knows by whom it was erected. It baffles the mind how ancient people could have moved the huge Stonehenge stones. The legend of King Arthur even comes into play in the discussion of the construction of Stonehenge. One Twelfth Century writer, Geoffrey of Monmouth, in his History of the Kings of Britain , wrote that Merlin brought the stones to the Salisbury Plain from Ireland sometime in the fifth century, and Merllin suggested an expedition to Ireland for the purpose of transplanting the "Giant's Ring Stone Circle" to Britain (stones that had been previously brought to Ireland from Africa by giants). Others suggest this was the work of extra-terrestrials; but no one really knows how Stonehenge was erected or what its purpose was. It is all speculation.

Award winning poet and author, Penelope Dyan and photographer John D. Weigand traveled to Stonehenge to bring this book to you and to remind us all that nothing is impossible, even if it seems that way. Stonehenge is proof positive of that!

Circle Of Stone
Bellissima Publishing, LLC

Circle Of Stone
A Kid's Guide To Stonehenge

Photography By John D. Weigand
Poetry By Penelope Dyan

Birds sit on top of the stone,
claiming Stonehenge as their own.

Sheep graze in the fields.
There are cattle nearby.
People stand looking at Stonehenge...
and wonder how and why.
How and why did this place come to be?
You see, it is a mystery.

Did King Arthur build this place?
Did our ancients come from outer space?
Or has man lost what he used to be
in this place of tranquility?
Some say it is quite clear
that the Druids worshipped here.
But no one will ever really know,
and our curiosity will continue to grow.

Here is one interesting fact.
Some rocks play a balancing act.

While others make an arch or a door.
And here is something; there is even MORE!

Look at the stones from another view.
And you will see something new.
Notice the stones, their placement in the sun.
Do they mark in heaven where time had begun?
Do the stones mark a special place
of a time in the universe or a time in space?

Some stones are small and some are big,
for an explanation. . . into history we dig.
It is said small stones began the construction.
And the larger stones came at a later junction.
We know this happened long ago,
because the archeologists tell us so.
And we know that by some it is often said,
this place was built to honor the dead.

We see a burial mound...

Then we see two. . .
We will see many more before we are through.

To honor the dead, this place rings true,
Because is that not what we would do?
We honor our fallen warriors today,
building monuments to them, a similar way.
We can see one tribute, the Vietnam Wall.
We honor the men that in that war did fall.
There we can read each and every name.
Isn't that really kind of the same?

We see two rocks taller than giraffes,
One seems to smile and so we laugh.

As we gaze at the circle, tried and true,
we wonder what it is that we would do.
Would we go to this place to pray,
if we traveled back in time some way?
And as we contemplate the mystery again,
of this place, and of how, why, who and when. . .
we remember (as impossible as this all seems)
that we can do anything if we follow our dreams.
Maybe that is WHY these stones now stand,
so majestic upon this land.

"There is no past that we can bring back by longing for it. There is only an eternally new now that builds and creates itself out of the Best as the past withdraws."

Johann Wolfgang Von Goethe (1749-1832)
German poet, novelist and dramatist.

www.ingramcontent.com/pod-product-compliance
Ingram Content Group UK Ltd.
Pitfield, Milton Keynes, MK11 3LW, UK
UKHW060132240426
12048UKWH00002B/11